A Life in Poetry

by

Hazel Campbell-Grant

Grosvenor House
Publishing Limited

This book is published by
Grosvenor House Publishing Ltd
28-30 High Street, Guildford, Surrey, GU1 3EL.
www.grosvenorhousepublishing.co.uk

A CIP record for this book
is available from the British Library

ISBN 978-1-78148-584-2

Dedicated to my loving family:

Especially to my husband Ian who has been my help and stay throughout our time together, without whom this book would not have been possible.

And to my beautiful daughters Emma and Catherine, always helpful, loving and affectionate.

And their families:

Simon,
Ewan,
James
and Zara

Grahame, Verity, Carmen and Elizabeth

Frustration

Shall I, can I, write a clever poem
with jingling rhymes,
teasing thoughts,
enigmatic to tangy finish?

Shall I, can I, write a poem
with deep meaning,
sonorous words,
to leave readers thoughtful,
pondering upon a wisdom?

Shall I, can I, write a poem
both clever and deep,
to give a satisfying whole?

Why is it,
when I think I have something to say,
cleverness is a dead art,
sonorous words evade me,
so the message is too blunt.........?

Contents

WAR AND PROTEST

BAD TIMES

A MIXTURE

SOME POEMS
IN DATE ORDER

A Day in Harrow

Dad cycles in early traffic
to the factory; machines leaf
paper around metal drums,

deafening the men gambling
with cards amidst giant bales.
The presses gobble up paper,

to be spat out as pamphlets
dropped behind enemy lines,
plans for D-day, ration-books.

The hooter sounds; at last
an end to the working day;
upstairs to the roof;

Dad's turn to fire watch; planes
threatening in the distance,
caterwauling of the siren;

At home and in the shelter
Mum faces another night
with four tiny children.

Events 1944

To Dad

A little girl of five,
three boisterous boys.
Who will go with daddy to buy the beach ball?
A ball is just a bauble to a girl
but sons and dad are soccer-mad.

The choice is made.

How proud the little girl;
how bright the ball
she carries in her hand.
A bond implanted,
enriching both their lives.

Events 1947

The Cremation

We drove in silence,
the hearse leading the way.
In the chapel the backdrop to prayers,
music, was the sound of sobbing.
I did not cry; as the coffin
started to move, jerking into action,
it made me laugh inside; Dad
with his infectious sense of humour
waving goodbye as he tripped
the light fantastic to the flames.
Never was a day so bright,
the sky so blue, the jokes
so funny, the food so tasty.

After, walking alone in the park,
I breathed through open mouth
to stop the tears, trying to share
the death of my father
with a lost God.

Events 1965
Written 2003

Bablock Hythe

I remember watery shadows
amidst noon's glowering heat;
mariners prompted to moor
at a jolly tavern; spied a cask,
from which flowed liquid gold,
frothing gently into the glasses
of the worshippers, reverently sipped;
a not so holy communion.

And I remember a boat reflected;
mariners tippling sleepily;
all around the despoils
of the day, bottles gorged
with the same mellifluous brew,
enriching sun with chuckling lights,
promising wanton pleasure,
and a day fulfilled.

Events 1973 on a Thames boat trip
when I discovered Real Ale.
Written 1995

Emma – 6 Months

A baby

entranced
by fingers, toes,

playing,
searching,

in butterfly thoughts
of an embryo mind,

playing with dreams,
searching for reality,

her dreams,
her reality.

1975

Communication

Through the babbling
an occasional word breaks out.
She is learning, she will learn
to mouth the platitudes of speech,
the same-said words repeated endlessly,
the human parrot cries.

But will that fluid body stiffen
whose every movement expressed a thought?
And will those speaking eyes go dumb?
Or will they make union with the tongue
to give more richly than before?

1976

A Walk in Bryce Canyon

*A memory of a trip to West and Central U.S.A with my family in 1988;
participants were Catherine 8, Emma 13, Hazel and Ian.*

The girls rushed to see inflamed rocks,
scramble around outcrops, engage with terrain.
We two strolled through arid magnificence,
the sun flaying our lightly-clad bodies.

Emma, always audacious,
began tip-toeing over a pool,
remains of a flash-flood,
rust-encrusted.

Catherine followed, but with jaunty step
until the surface cracked.
Sliding into underlying mud, she fell,
legs, clothes, camera, all smeared scarlet.

I turned on Emma, scolding;
she gaped with astonishment;
thoughtlessness her only crime,
the offender obviously Catherine.

Ian cheered on the bedraggled girl;
she clambered erect,
panicked for path,
the mire grasping at her feet.

Safely retrieved, we scrubbed at her
with maternal-spittled hankies;
the bog resisted like glue;
we trailed back, a desultory crew.

Emma's Poem

Family Folklore

(After "Daddy fell into the pond" by Alfred Noyes.)

The rocks bled. It was a hot, strong day.
We were strolling along an arid way.
Everybody was chewing the cud
When
Catherine fell into the mud.

Mum began scolding with sheer surprise.
We gazed in delight, not believing our eyes.
Daubed in scarlet from head to toe,
The bog dragged her down; she had nowhere to go.

Cheered on by Dad, who was safe on the path,
She gave the impression she needed a bath.
Clambering erect, staggering for safety,
Her feet splayed out, she was in no way stately.
We laughed out loud; she looked such a dud
When
Catherine fell into the mud.

Alice, Gift from Nature and Mankind

In loving memory of Alice

Nature's grandeur, manifested
in a universe vast beyond imagination,
by spheres singing in their courses,
through prodigality of planetary life,
culminates in the miracle
of a newborn child.

Mankind's genius, expressed
by astronauts leaping on the moon,
in the profundity of Shakespeare,
finds compassion in the miracle
of saving a hydrocephalic child
with a shunt to drain fluids.

Alice, miraculous was your birth,
miraculous your beginning,
a gift from nature and mankind,
your personality warm and glowing
as if the gods reached out
to help you on your way.

The shunt blocked, your brain
drowned, death took you away,
just as the promise
of your childhood
aspired to maturity.

You remain a symbol of hope;
mankind and nature can unite
giving life and joy to the world,
our stumbling steps may yet become
a loving walk with nature.

Events 1990
Written 1995

A Day Like Any Other Day

Working at my desk, window open,
I feel the road slowly grow hectic
with heat and children playing.
Across the way a last-ditch batsman
exits to exuberant clamour. Next door
a garden sprinkler entices water-fights.
An effervescent queue races to form
at calls from an ice-cream van.
Bike-bells ring as wheels flash by.
Teenagers preen on the corner.
A holiday like any other holiday.

The phone rings.
    ..accident
   ..come   ..now
  ..sunlight   ..noise   ..recede
   ..moving   ..automaton
   ..damned   ..seat-belt
  ..driving   ..fast
    ..swing-park
   ..child   ..dazed
  ..ambulance

A hospital like any other.

The day Catherine broke both
her arms 1990. Written 1996.

Breakup

One day my husband married another.
We parted on his adultery; neither
could think of any other reason.
Happily I became single, with
a couple of daughters, job, to mind.

Picking up the girls, he said
"she's gone", asked me out,
his mind yoyoing from sorrow
to hope in one breath.
I thought "why not", replied
"getting back a no-no of course".

Our discourse renewed: hilarity
resurrected with private jokes
old, new. The girls delighted
in mastering the Goons, kindled
at Oscar Wilde, revelled
with Monty Python, but we had
conjoined in laughter over the years,
it was just his glad eye had divided us.

Looking back on breakup 1990.
Written 2004

To My Anorexic Daughter

You are to me a gift beyond understanding,
life, body, soul, cause of delight
and inexpressible joy.

But when you despise that life and body,
when your soul is primed to self-destruct
I weep within.

Please think again,
let my tears wash away your self-contempt,
my yearnings resurrect your soul
to a new beginning.

1993

Night Watch

Evil mires the night; trees loom;
brick walls rear intangible beasts;
bushes stretch to lacerate and maul;
malign vapours ooze around cars,
Stygian ferryboats navigating void;
lights conflict, skew burning shadows.

A coach arrives.
Children swarm.
Engines spark.
Headlights stare.
School buildings wake.
Gloom scatters.

Yet, in residual night
are those that creep, slime-encrusted,
back to eternal screaming caverns.

Picking Catherine up from
Luckley Oakfield School.
1994

To Kate

A quiet presence next to me at work,
sweetly feminine but discriminating,
your intelligence fuelling gentle wit;

always first to see the joke,
your laughter intermittent through the day,
your happiness infecting all you meet;

finding the best in everyone and everything,
your warm greetings trigger confidences
to a ready listener.

And when you are alone,
remember the goodwill
that surrounds you like a cloak
from the friendships of the years,
I am only one who loves you
for your kindness and charity.

No more working from home – and a new friend!
1994

I Love

quarrelling over the housework,
arguments about neglected studies,
the clash of the generations.

listening to happy voices on the phone,
shuddering when the bill arrives,
the ready assumption of a bottomless purse.

the parties,
hilarity and music till the small hours,
worrying about the neighbours.

the visits,
going to cook lasagne and finding no pasta,
needing to dash to the shops but the car is gone,
washing machine overworked,
tumble-dryer monopolised.

the departures,
cupboards raided,
soups and spaghetti swanning out the door.

And I love their love,
the pure love of youth
that spills over, rejuvenating me.

Northcott
1995

Souvenir of Winchester

My birthday trip:
Emma, down from University,
Catherine, the younger,
Ian and I, divorced, making group complete,
a family reunited for just one day.

Sometimes we are shoppers,
a serious affair, disregarding cold
to ransack shops, bags accumulating.

Sometimes we are refugees,
fleeing cold to inn or cafe,
coats jumbled onto chair and floor,
food voraciously consumed.

Always we are tourists,
stumbling on beam-etched buildings,
fragments of ruins; this legendary city
is imprinted by the rise and fall of kings:
great Alfred, the fabled Round Table
of Arthur are among the memorials here;
at the heart a wondrous cathedral bears witness
to a people's struggle to transcend itself,
sky-borne arches inspire to the sublime,
carry us beyond our divided present.

1995

"The Gang's All Here"

Nobody could believe the news,
Celeste, of the six, was hurt.
Traversing the miles,
five met in dismal reunion
by the coma-quiet room.

We parents worried at home,
the sweet fresh face memorable on mind.
Ghosts of children past came to haunt us......

Lively laughter rang through the house.
Silhouettes were seen on the garage roof
giggling at discovery.
A snooker ball smashed table-top,
and a line of upright innocents
leant against a wall reading magazines.
Videos were repeatedly watched,
teenage movies, past family events,
antique episodes of John Steed.
There were sleepovers with floor-covered bedding,
midnight feasts surreptitiously consumed.

In the heat of summer
helter-skelter went the water-fights!
A map grew amid excitement
as a computer game daily unravelled.

Slowly the news was good,
Celeste, of the six, was making progress,
once more, "the gang's all here".

Looking back at growing up in Octavia
Written 1999

Sitting on a Rock in Aberglaslyn

Below, the rabid torrent races,
creator and destroyer of this mountain pass;
tumult engulfs birdsong,
muffles motors rolling in rocky cleft.
Bushes and trees battle for space, roots
claw at heights, rear out of pools;
branches contest; winter-skeletal against
fresh green sprinkled against khaki needled;
clashing, suffocating, drowning;
new-come rhododendrons valley hang.
Ubiquitous moss is patchworked
with composting leaves, fungal lavas,
insect debris. Turmoil in the midst
torments boulders to rocks to pebbles.

And in my mind are whirls and eddies
of past visits with past people.

*Looking back at holidays in Bryn Bychan
in North Wales.   Written 1999*

Love Gifts

I lean back to delight in your new gift,
"Daughter of Africa",
erect, slim, draped luminous scarlet,
colour matched across the stony fireplace,
where tenderness frames mother and child.

Above is Imladris, boulder-strewn,
green-misted, where elves are chronicled
to have built Rivendell ; and you knelt
contemptuous of the torrent
to dedicate our love.

Cards jostle on the mantelpiece, rejoicing in our marriage.
Half-hidden behind, blue-robed angels soar
in a gold background, remembrance of junk shops
ransacked; pity like a newborn babe rises
on printed cardboard, a Blake memento from the Tate.

At the top, first buy for our home, an oriental dragon
is traced by silver threads, oak-surrounded;
others in gilded white porcelain and vibrant crystal,
rampage on shelves; painted brash red and green,
a toy dragon simpers in one corner.

At the centre Buddha meditates, transforming
these love-gifts of our life together into prayers of joy.

Remarrying Ian 2002

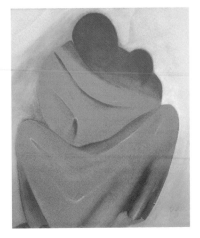

The Pub Garden

Under a tree animated by a breeze
we sit, each with glass in hand,
on benches we have occupied many times.
We are rare visitors now, regulars then,
when the pub lay on the road
to his parents' house.

Our children toddled these paths,
delighted in the winged-beat
of those swings, attended
by their indulgent Granny; while
Grandpa chatted and chuckled,
his moustache jovial with beer froth.

Now we pause between the two generations,
one striding out to start life, the other
a memory, their home gone. This garden
is hallowed as a church, ghosts
young and old, rise from the stones.

2003

Growing Up

I mull over mirror, a sigh escapes;
try to forget fat-landscaped back;
melon breasts rolling to rotund belly.
My eyes travel up to turkey neck,
furrowed face, eyes black-ringed,
hair iron grey, patched silver.

Memories-a girl walks with lilting step,
feels slender, lissom,
finds choosing impeded,
garment after garment vitalised,
jokes "a good clothes-hanger";
careless, young, complete.

Where has that girl gone?

Carried away to the land of hard knocks.
What remains?
Gifts of love received along the way.

2010

To Catherine

Beloved,
I have lived you
in the troubled days,
and I have loved you
through the happy hours.
You, more than anyone,
have been tested
on your way through life;
though I tried to help
I fear I was not always
equal to the task, so it
has been a lonely path
you travelled.

Hence I have found great joy
these last few years to see
your courage rewarded,
and to watch the flowering
of your personality. You
always said yes to life,
love, and, as a just result,
have finally found happiness
in your loving family, Grahame,
Verity, Carmen and Elizabeth.

2011

A Visit to Aberglaslyn

We have taken the path to the rabid river;
creator, destroyer, of this mountain pass.
Once more Ian, Emma, Catherine, will attempt
to conquer these falls, this time
with cousins Alison, Hannah. We trample
through mud around trees, negotiating
zigzag paths patchworked with forest debris.
The girls look out for a way onto the rocks.

Trees battle for territory. Roots claw
at heights. Occasional cones caught in rocks
signal pine trees spiky in the fitful canopy;
spring finery graces branches; others
form a tracery melancholy brown; everywhere
are rhododendrons, mature green leaves,
flowers coming into bud. The Beddgelert road
descends, winding beside the torrent.
The lay-by is here, where we met Granny,
Grandpa on many North Wales holidays;
the famous episode, "spider with finger nails"
caused much laughter, tickling.

I climb to get a view; above tumult,
shout a temporary goodbye. The assault

begins; finding stepping stones,
handholds with difficulty, they clamber
onto boulders, leaping from one
to another, at any moment risking a slip
into the water teeming past. Going on two,
three boulders with joyous alleluias,
before the way is barred by a wider gap
between rocks, causing a reluctant
diversion. So on, sometimes retreating
to the bank, starting again further down;
until they tire of the adventure.

Finally we meet where the rapids
drop under a narrow bridge, junction
of three roads. By family custom we stop
here to take farewell of the stream.
We race to be first, forming a line,
leaning over the wall, gazing into water,
lost in whirls and eddies of past visits,
past people, a kaleidoscope of time.

Final version of Aberglaslyn poem
Finished 2010

Grey breakers clash

Grey breakers clash,
heaving out of the depths
tons of violent sea.
The girl watches the turmoil,
exhilarated by the unbridled
power of waves crashing
to their deaths, destroyed
in a moment to cascades
of white foam, transformed
to scuttling sea creatures
finally absorbed by rippling
sand only to sink back before
the rhythmic assault
of subsequent seas.

Grey mountainous tides merge
into embattled clouds
of yesteryear, hurry away
the seasons, scudding
on into the future,
carrying away the young girl,
thrilling to the grandeur
and pomp of sky-driven storms.

Leaving an aged lady,
shaken by life's tempests
receiving daily intimations
of cold death. Remembering
childhood storms, dreaming
of the peace of sunshine
after the deluge.

2012

LOVE AND FAITH

The Mountain of Truth

*"Those who follow their own consciences are of my religion and
I am of the same religion as those who are good and brave"* –
Henri IV of France

Fight
to love;
do not pamper
your comfortable faith,
which does not allow
the beliefs of others.

Climb
your path,
and kindly watch over
those on other paths.

Faith
must live with love
else become destruction.

1998

Love and Faith

'God is love'
If this were so then all faiths
would have a happy acceptance
of each other. But faiths,
old and new, vie for supremacy,
create another tower of Babel,
and screams of people crucified are not heard,
and the quiet love of God is not felt.

2010

Thoughts

Let us not worship
the god of false unselfishness,
but each lean on each
to grow together towards maturity.

And let us not judge or forgive,
but thoughtlessly accept
as happy children do.

1988

Gathered Together in Another Name

The Koran relates how Hagar,
alone with her dying baby son
in the desert, searching,
desperate for water, cried
for the compassion of Allah;
Gabriel stamped his heel,
a stream was torn from the rock.

Immaculate from this source,
carried to a suburban house
in England; Muslims pray,
turning to Mecca;
Christians, agnostics
subside into reverence,
all drink down the draught.

Hatha yoga classes are active
every Thursday; after practising
physical exercises
with mindful attention,
meditations give insights
into the rites of mankind
and universal goodness.

At the Buddhist meeting
conducted in a church hall,
a likeness of Christ overlooks
hallowed images of Tibet,
as if Jesus is present,
blessing this group, gathered
together in another name.

2003

To Aldous Huxley
The Perennial Philosophy

My youthful mind wormed through book
upon book, searched religion
after religion, seeking worldwide,
until it found your book and rested.

To me the culmination of your life's work,
evolved over many years by studying
enlightened works of holy men
from all nations and cultures.

A philosophy gleaned from the great religions
that serve the world; higher than all
is mysticism, the stem nourishing every faith,
unifying, not dividing; extracts
speak of selfless love, God-centred souls.

But this is more than anthology;
though you quote the wise,
your voice is wiser yet,
this exposition of the Way
interprets and illuminates.

Within the pages is no talk
of a new faith to contend
with old, but ancient wisdoms
and quiet philosophical voice.

The tattered paperback
with yellowed leaves,
costing five shillings,
is all the world to me.

2004

To Chopin

Your melodies
are wordless thoughts
deep in my existence,
each note satisfies
and embraces my being,
conjuring to a pinnacle
of unspeakable sorrow,
unspeakable joy,
both not one, but the other,
so I cannot choose between,
rising to the sublime.

1985

WAR AND PROTEST

Peace

They say peace has come to Derry,
love is in Belfast,
but the marchers keep on marching,
and stones are flying fast.

Doves coo in churches
where the entrenched faithful pray,
but hate still rends their hearts,
and drives the peace away.

At school they read the Bible,
declaring love and peace to all,
but not to children down the road
taught in another school.

They say peace has come to Derry,
love is in Belfast,
but the marchers keep on marching,
and stones are flying fast.

2005

Peace2

Ronan Kerr, a Catholic policeman,
has been blown up by a bomb.
His mother calls for Catholics
to continue joining the police.
And the leaders of Northern Ireland
are "united" in condemnation
of the horrid act. Martin McGuiness
"stands up to be counted"
in support of Catholics in the police.
Peter Robinson also gives his backing
to a force offering a service to all
the people, Protestant or Catholic.
So each pointless tragedy transforms
into a hard-won step forward
by the people of the North.

2011

War in Iraq

1

March Against War

Straight off the train, onto the demonstration,
a serpent moving through the streets
of the capital. We come, mother, daughters
to protest. Around us, a throng of people,
representatives of many cultures, nations,
religions, generations, join with camaraderie
to say: this country with all its pretensions
to civilisation, should draw back from this
illegal attack. Two flows merge, the thoroughfare
becomes a river of bodies, throwing out waves
of stamping, shouting, to the helicopters above;
the squeal of whistles, sold by the way,
adds to the cacophony; banners, placards lurch
alarmingly, defy gravity. The day draws on;
we take time out from the creeping advance in a cafe;
back to this jumble of humanity, single-minded,
purposeful. Daylight fades; most of the crowd
have missed the speeches; disperse duty done.

2

War Over Baghdad on TV

The thrum of bombers; in the distance
is a full-scale 1812 overture;
fireworks dagger the sky; cannon
thump with bravado; the orchestra
crescendos with explosions.

Superimposed overall is the murmuring
of statistics from the American military;
types of plane, heights of over-flight,
types of bomb, designated targets, sizes
of bomb, possible "collateral casualties";
cutting to technical diagrams,
clinical aides memoirs; Baghdad
is the object of gunnery practice.

3
On TV Again

There is carnage in a market
in Baghdad, another errant missile.
While the newsreader drones on,
a man with his head encased
in bloody rags, is passed
from anxious hand to anxious hand,
repeatedly; a puzzle arises,
"collateral casualties" were high,
among them many children, where
have all these pictures gone?
Dispassionately the voice explains:
the film is too horrific to show us,
the perpetrators. Nevertheless
it has been shown in Egypt,
Syria, many Muslim countries.

2003

BAD TIMES

Please miss this out if you don't like angst.
I put it in for completeness, for my husband and two daughters.

Hospital – First Stay

1
My first stay in any hospital.
I watch television.
Looking around, everybody else has gone.
I only remain.
And the nurses.
I enter the night ward.
See a light, quieted by a shroud.
Hear stertorous breathing,
as if my father died again.
All around is gasp and shift.
Wretchedly I turn my head;
no empty bed to view;
bodies cage me
in fright I escape.
To the waiting nurses.
Adamant, I must go back;
my manic mind speaks in rebellion,
outside I watch.

Six nurses from nowhere.
Grabbing me.
Dragging me.
Pinning me down.
I react.
I start to fight back.
I struggle.

They struggle.
Teaching me to fight them.
Teaching me not to give in.

2
The nurse shakes me.
I wake reluctantly from doped sleep.
I want to sleep; I need to sleep.
I must not argue.
Go into the washroom.
I pass out, cracking my head on stone.
Later I think "over-worked and underpaid,
nothing more to be said"
Later still, they tell my mother
I split my head falling out of bed.

3
Another injection.
The nurses converge.
I struggle; I fight;
Sister shouts
"Get it in anywhere"
Needle pierces my thigh.
For days I limp.
They taught me to fight.
They taught me never to give in.

4

I have a theory; some of us,
too good for this obscene world
take refuge in madness;
such is the sweet lady
I count my friend.
Sitting down, I begin to chatter;
receiving no response, I turn:
she sits erect, with eyes
mute to sense, saliva
curdling from vacuous mouth.
Suddenly aware, I look up;
a nurse quickly turns away;
returning, I gaze in horror;
I cannot even guess at her offence
to have been so doused with drugs.

5

Grouped in laughter, talking, chatting,
the grey-haired figure lonely in the midst,
the congealed plate of food;
the tube, significant on table;
teenage voices hound
"Eat up Gran or………"
teenage fingers point,
the tube threatening on table
the old lady, mind-lost, storm-toss'd.

My throat thickened.

6

Late again; a nurse smiles;
surprised, her kind looks overcome me.
Another injection.
I stand patiently.
Alone, I panic.
I have been tricked.
I must not sleep.
running to the washroom
I hold a door, walking on the spot.
She comes; she smiles;
I am pliant again;
she leads me to bed.

I wake with beating head;
hands shaking coffee out of the cup.

7

The night nurses make their rounds.
All falls quiet.
The tossing and broken breath
of wakefulness calm.
The nurses march.
Anyone discerned as watchful
will be injected.
All must be at rest.
So the night nurses can sleep.

8

I pass a nurse in the passage.
She smiles.
I smile back.
They think I don't remember
violence and neglect.
But I'll hate them till I die.
I'll never give in.

9

Epilogue
Time has kindly dimmed the past.
But when the sick pain of depression
grips the pit of my stomach
I live these scenes again,
and all is negativity.

Events 1969

A Prayer

Thou
who know the deep dark,
who love the deeply sinning,
come now to me.

I
who love not,
who most deeply sin,
where can I find forgiveness
if not in Thee.

I am lost.
The storm rages.
The deep dark encloses me round.

Still
I must go on,
the end is not in sight.

I
who hunger for the end
will not yet be filled.

Thou,
who know my end,
keep me through the dark.

Written at the height of a nervous breakdown 1970

Hospital – Second Stay

1

It is a punishment.
I said I was fine too often,
but so I was:
only every day I drooped with drugs,
I could not do my job.
One day the doctor stopped the drugs
and ended all. Six months later
I entered that dread place again.

2

Another battle.
Inevitable injection.
I do not ask myself why I fight.
It has become a habit.
I refuse tea.
The nurses laugh.

3

I wake to half-light.
My tongue cleaves to roof of my mouth.
In thin nightie and bare feet
I go in search of water:
into the day ward, past sleeping nurses,
along the corridor, trying doors
until I find the kitchen, glass,
pour water, drink. I may need it again,

carrying the glass I return
past unmoving nurses; my illness
is so extreme they force and beat me,
but not so extreme they
need to care for me as nurses should.
Clambering aboard the bed,
the glass slips to the floor,
into smithereens.
I am done, the drugs take over.

I wake to glass crunching underfoot,
a day nurse has found my glass.
Later I wonder; glass sharp on wet floor,
my dehydration; if I had risen again
in thin nightie and bare feet,
what the consequences?

Events 1970

Depression

Despair.
Deep down.
No hope left.
All options gone.
Fantasise, circling on death.
Black depths of total inadequacy,
of total uselessness,
grind my mind down to helpless sorrow.
No way open, save the fall
into a pit of weeping anguish,
the only solution, total oblivion.

1970

Paranoia

Perhaps it's a joke;
life is grovelling in a pit
of pain and anguish,
in a world tired with famine war disaster,
an earth reeking with the stench
of man's inhumanity to man.
Perhaps life's God's joke,
and,
maybe,
one day,
we'll all wake laughing because we understand,
maybe,
one day.

1970

Thoughts on Van Gogh's Cornfield

Black crows eddy golden corn,
the path leads to blank future
in yesterday's tortured mind,
falling into death's abyss.

Black crows shadow gold-flowered gorse,
echo back past pain,
let go, let go, the rooky wood,
life renews itself and so must we,
the path leads on
to today's living sunshine.

1998

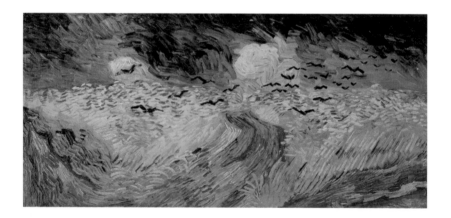

A MIXTURE

Twilight on the South Bank

The river is crimped and tousled,
by wind, tide; boats garnished
with lights, are locked to the banks,
or busy homewards in the urban glow.

Olive-leaved trees stand sentinel
along the slab-edged stream,
interspersed with antique lamps,
muted by dazzle of fluorescence.

Up here, on the fifth floor
of the Festival Hall,
only murmuring rises from below,
but for the heavy thudding of trains
snaking over Charing Cross bridge.

Against blood-tinged clouds
is jagged silver of a walkway,
the span almost hidden by workers
scurrying, aiming for the suburbs,
vanishing into the Underground.

Then celebrants make their way
to this concrete jungle
of the best theatres, cinemas,
concert halls, restaurants.

As night falls, these palaces
of entertainment create a medley
of sound fragments dancing
above the listening river.

2004

Housework

The daily round of clear and tidy,
no sooner a video viewed,
than it must be picked up, put away.

The weekly round of dust and hoover,
furniture to be polished,
ornaments brightened.

> It's better to get on with life;
> you can't always be worrying
> about the last dirty cup.

> There are books to read,
> gardens to excavate,
> revolutions to plan.

> In a properly disordered house
> what fun may be found in a heap
> thrown by the side of a bed.

> Those discarded magazines
> on the arm of a chair
> are always ready for retrieval.

The greatest treat of all
is climbing into work clothes
to vanquish a room's layered chaos.

Such an adventure of sorting,
so much scything through dust,
such revelation of white paint,

until pristine again
the room shines for days,
proudly perfect for a moment.

2004

Strangers on a Shifting Bed Lie Unquiet

Watched from a speeding train, urban sprawl,
rivers, forests, villages hypnotise.

Abruptly out of green fertility
a stony crop arises, graves
isolated in rural calm,
bereft of church, of any building.
Do the dead mourn organ's music,
listen still for creak of lych-gate?

The sea with avid persistence
preys upon a village; then the dead
are scrambled onto rocks, somersault
with tides, plummet into depths;
strangers on a shifting bed lie unquiet.

A city church is pressed for space,
centuries of death and decay remove
from crypt to rural churchyard; carbon-dating
the bones competes with parish records,
a useful exercise for the living.
The dead are in agony from bones-grind.

A town church converts to warehouse;
its graves lie wantonly pillaged,
degraded, forlorn. The dead
were torn out screaming, deposed
to inferior lodgings. Do they
tremble now at the chunter of trucks?

2004

Reality

'Breathe deeply.'
The mask came down.

The day was pleasant.
The sun shone.
'Good morning'
breezed the receptionist.
The dentist smiled a welcome.
'Breathe deeply.'
The mask came down.

I awoke.
Or did I?
Or am I in some other reality
still at the dentist?

1962

Novice Gardener

In the helter-skelter
of child-rearing, life-digging,
no time to delve a garden
watch petals open.

In the quiet of later years
a novice gardener sets to work,
cutting back, clearing,
uncovering treasures buried

in leaves, choked with weeds.
She redesigns borders, noses
through books, sets out shrubs,
until now their names unknown.

Next year she learns the year,
prunes with book to hand;
each plant in turn comes into season,
replete with bee and hoverfly.

Hot August, earth unyielding,
she watches the blackbirds nesting
in the ivy; her eyes survey
a garden coming into existence;

plants in ordered chaos, trees
whirlpools of shifting green, birds
careering in a lattice-work
of branches.

She looks back upon a journey,
feels herself slowly flowering.

2004

Relaxation

About to be busy.
Stopped.
Cat, throat-throbbing, on my lap.

Eyes sink into night-eyes, impassive, mystic;
fingers sink into fur, eroded, tongue-silk;
flesh shrinks from claws, naked, ecstatic.

Relaxing
into quiet stroking,
the world can wait awhile...

1987

This Colour

is the pallor on a sick child's face;
is Grandma's carpet where we go for tea;
is a road more major than red;
is a dragon with fire in his belly;
is a land gripped by Arctic seas;
is envy of another's good fortune;
is immature, naive to the extreme;
is a frog, muddy in a puddle;
is the face of Tara, Holy Mother Buddha;
is mould on ancient bread;
is seaweed clambering over wet rocks;
is immature sedum like broccoli flowering;
is unripe tomatoes, fried to perfection;
is chlorophyll, life-giver to the planet;
is the Channel on a sunny day;
is emeralds on a radiant girl's finger;
is verdant pasture, with deposits of cow-pat;
is herbs, giving charisma to a casserole;
is salad, lettuce, cucumber, avocado;
is Spring after the dead of Winter;
is pine trees dark against bright snow;
is leaves shimmering in the wind;
is GO.

2004

Toon Town

Crash!

Paper-thin cat
irrepressibly
bounces back

taking vengeance
on chortling mouse
thrown over cliff

to face temporary
annihilation
in his turn;

clownish humour
carried
to extremity

in a merry
-go-round
of catastrophe.

My children
laugh, no need
for "Are you okay?"

in bloodless
painless
destruction.

1998

Evolution

Once   with mammoth limbs, gargantuan body
            I was locked to earth.
Now   I climb the sky with tiny wings,
            abseil down the wind.

Once   my reptilian yell sweltered
            in pre-Cambrian swamps.
Now   I blow bubbles of song,
            chirrup in branches.

Once   I stumped ungainly through mud,
            mashing plants and creepers.
Now   I hop light as a sunbeam,
            soar from bough to bough.

Once   my clammy blood was warmed
            by scales baked in the sun.
Now   my body ferments
            its own restless energy.

Once   tropical heat
            swaddled my giant eggs.
Now   ,small and delicate, they
            are cuddled by my pulsing down,
And   give life to my young
            millions of years in the making.

2004

Mars

Cats barred in the kitchen;
garden snowed to a wilderness;
I climb to the comfort of my bedroom.

Elsewhere dawn kindles; alarm clocks
wake early risers; coffee,
breakfast are hastily consumed.

In another country, holidaymakers
guard their bodies from noonday sun,
eat guavas, pawpaw, passion fruit.

Events made synchronous
by spinning Earth
looping in its orbit.

On another planet,
with different spin,
alternative orbit,
at the same moment,
Earthly wheels make marks.

2005

Space Travel – Before and After

See a coffee stained painting: where desert,
spikes, succulents, candy-floss mountains,
fashion into a comic-book-alien wilderness;
central is a cigar spaceship buttressed by fins
embracing the back-burn of the engine.
Gung-ho nearby, a spaceman displays a suit
contouring his heroic body, brandishes a gun,
eager to tangle with this ebullient world.
A huge, stone planet, fully lit,
rises above the horizon, in a black sky
dense with stars, orbs, a comet.

Radio waves pulse through space
to transform into TV pictures:
now see the Apollo lunar module,
an indeterminate machine
hung about with scientific instruments,
decorated with office-chair legs,
taking off from a bombed rock-scape.
Cavernous space backdrops a half-globe
lively in the distance,
wrapped in sunny blue seas,
straddled by swirling clouds,
Mother Earth sending out her young.

2010

Acknowledgements

Some of these poems have previously appeared in the publications ENVOI and ORBIS.

CPSIA information can be obtained
at www.ICGtesting.com
Printed in the USA
LVIC080133220213
3392LVUK00003B

* 9 7 8 1 7 8 1 4 8 5 8 4 2 *